Origami
PAPER & MEGA PACK

**MORE THAN 990 SHEETS OF ORIGAMI PAPER
PLUS BASIC FOLD INSTRUCTIONS**

FALL RIVER PRESS

New York

FALL RIVER PRESS

New York

An Imprint of Sterling Publishing
387 Park Avenue South
New York, NY 10016

STERLING INNOVATION and the distinctive Sterling Innovation logo are
registered trademarks of Sterling Publishing Co., Inc.

Cover design by The Book Designers
Interior design by Scott Russo

Paper patterns: Central Coast Pictures/Amy Joseph, Depositphotos, Dreamstime,
Ingram Publishing, istockphoto, Shutterstock

ISBN 978-1-4351-4480-4

Distributed in Canada by Sterling Publishing
c/o Canadian Manda Group, 165 Dufferin Street
Toronto, Ontario, Canada M6K 3H6
Distributed in the United Kingdom by GMC Distribution Services
Castle Place, 166 High Street, Lewes, East Sussex, England BN7 1XU
Distributed in Australia by Capricorn Link (Australia) Pty. Ltd.
P.O. Box 704, Windsor, NSW 2756, Australia

For information about custom editions, special sales, and premium and corporate purchases, please contact
Sterling Special Sales at 800-805-5489 or specialsales@sterlingpublishing.com.

Manufactured in China

2 4 6 8 10 9 7 5 3 1

Contents

Origami Symbols

Mountain fold

Mountain crease

Valley fold

Valley crease

VALLEY FOLD:
Fold paper forward

When you open paper that has been valley-folded, you will see a concave crease that bends inward like a groove, or valley. This is called a valley crease.

MOUNTAIN FOLD:
Fold paper backward

When you open paper that has been mountain-folded, you will see a convex crease that bends outward—it has a little peak you can pinch. This is called a mountain crease.

Fold toward you (valley fold) and in direction of arrow.

 Fold away from you (mountain fold) and in direction of arrow.

  Fold and unfold

 Insert

 Unfold

  Cut along line

 Curve paper (soft crease)

X-ray view

4

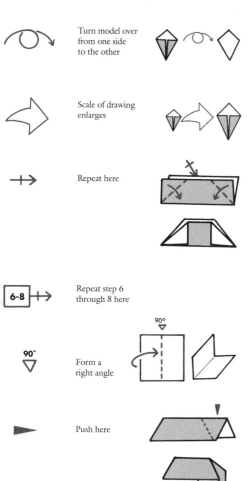

Turn model over from one side to the other

Scale of drawing enlarges

→→ Repeat here

6-8 →→ Repeat step 6 through 8 here

90° ▽ Form a right angle

► Push here

○ Hold here

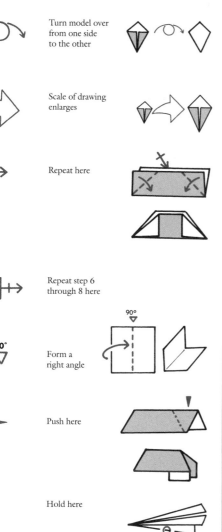

Rotate paper one half turn (top of model will rotate to bottom)

Rotate paper one quarter turn (top of model will rotate to side)

Rotate paper one eighth turn (top of model will rotate to side)

•⌒→• Match the dots

Raw Edge

Crease

Folded Edge

Double Raw Edge

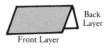

Back Layer

Front Layer

5

Basic Folds

BOOK FOLD

Fold one side edge over to lie on opposite side edge.

DIAPER FOLD

Fold one corner to lie over opposite corner.

CUPBOARD FOLD

Fold two opposite parallel sides towards each other to meet at center.

ICE CREAM CONE FOLD

Fold two adjacent sides to meet at center.

HOUSE ROOF FOLD

Fold two adjacent corners to meet at center.

BLINTZ FOLD

Fold all four corners to meet at center.

Note: Although less easily recognizable, the crease pattern for a sideways ice cream cone fold is still called an "ice cream cone fold." The same is true for all the basic folds.

Still an ice cream cone fold.

Still a book fold.

Still a cupboard fold.

Reverse Folds

Inside Reverse Fold

In order for you to perform a reverse fold, your model or portion of model should have a front layer, a back layer, and a folded edge or spine connecting the two layers. In a reverse fold, an end of this double layer of paper is turned either into itself (inside reverse fold) or around itself (outside reverse fold).

1 You may wish to prepare your paper first by performing a simple valley fold that will serve as a precrease.

2 Check to be sure this is the shape you would like the paper to ultimately take, then unfold.

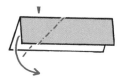

3 Spread the layers of your paper apart. Apply pressure (push in) at the mountain folded edge (spine) until it changes to a valley fold. At the same time, the precreases you made earlier will both become mountain folded edges.

4 This shows the inside reverse fold in progress. Keep applying pressure to end of paper until model can be flattened.

5 One end of your double layer is now "sandwiched" between the front and back layers.

Outside Reverse Fold

Again, starting with front and back layers connected by a "spine," you can "wrap" one end around both layers, as if turning a hood onto your head.

1 Mark the place where you want the fold to be (precrease). Unfold.

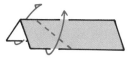

2 Spread the layers apart and wrap end around outside of model.

3 Press flat.

FOLDING HINTS

- It is usually easier to fold paper on a hard surface such as a table.

- Fold as neatly and as accurately as you can.

- If the paper you are using is colored or patterned on one side only: origami directions usually specify which side should be facing up when you begin folding. If this is not indicated, it is usually safe to begin with the white side of the paper facing you.

- It is usually easier to fold paper by bringing an edge from the lower part of the paper up. If you find it easier to fold this way and directions indicate a side-to-side or downward fold, you can always rotate your paper so that the direction of the fold is now upward, and then fold. After folding, reposition your paper so that it looks like the next step in the diagram.

- It is usually easier to make a valley fold in your model than to make a mountain fold. A valley fold becomes a mountain fold when you turn your paper over, so if a diagram indicates to make a mountain fold, you may choose to turn the paper over and make a valley fold. When you turn your paper back to the right side, you will see the desired mountain fold.

- Origami diagrams are usually drawn as if the paper were held loosely rather than pressed flat. This slightly three-dimensional representation is used to give you information about the different layers of paper. If you see a slight gap between edges in a diagram, this would disappear if model were pressed flat.

- In general, your paper should be folded right to an edge or crease, *without* leaving a gap, unless otherwise indicated in the written instructions.

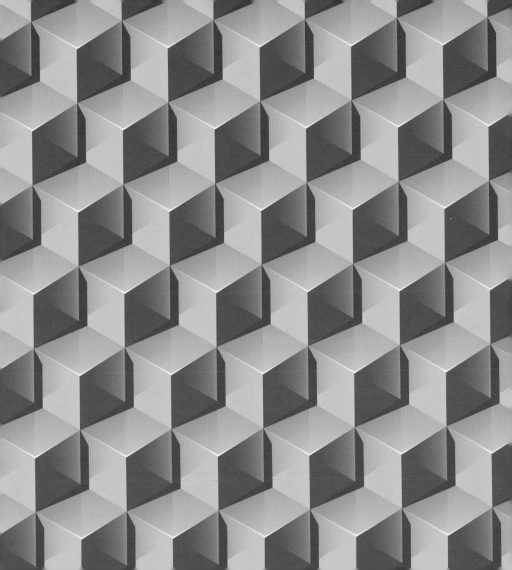

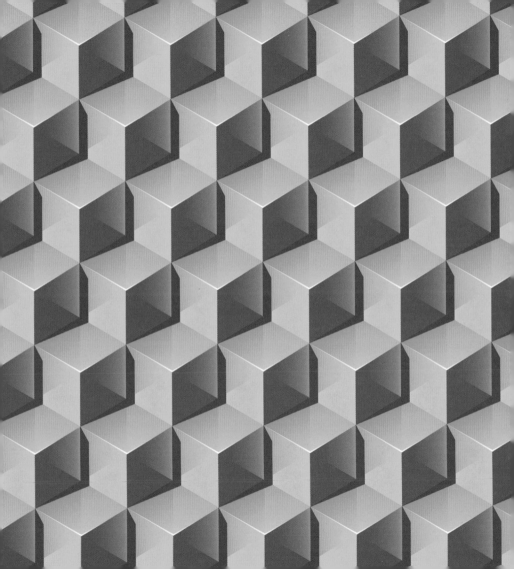

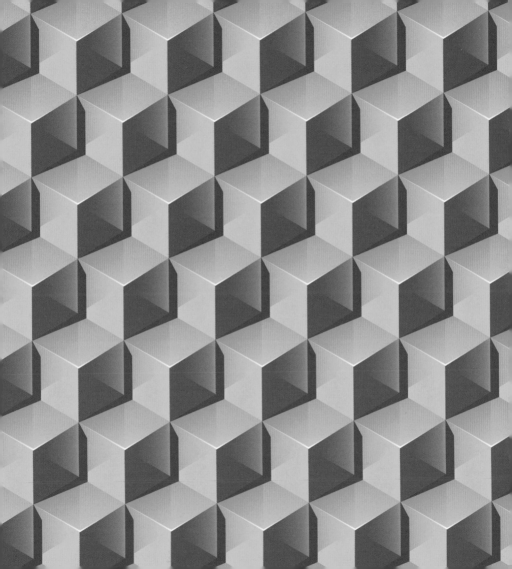

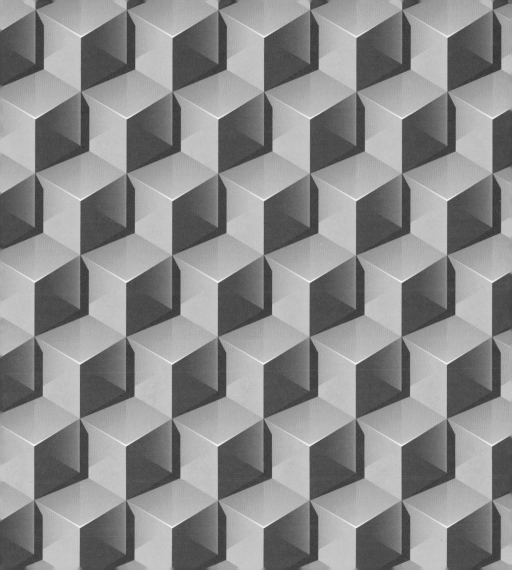

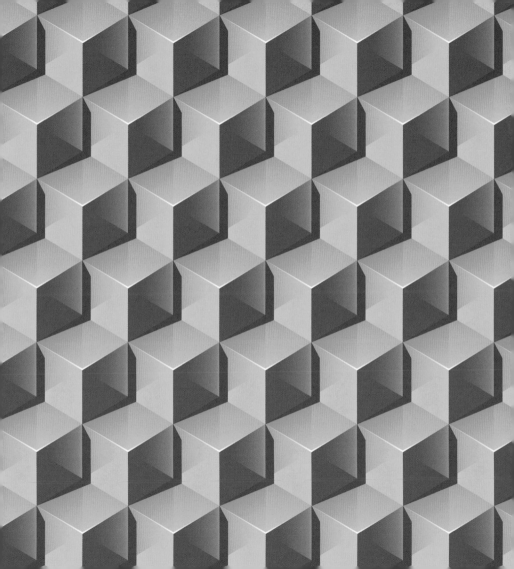

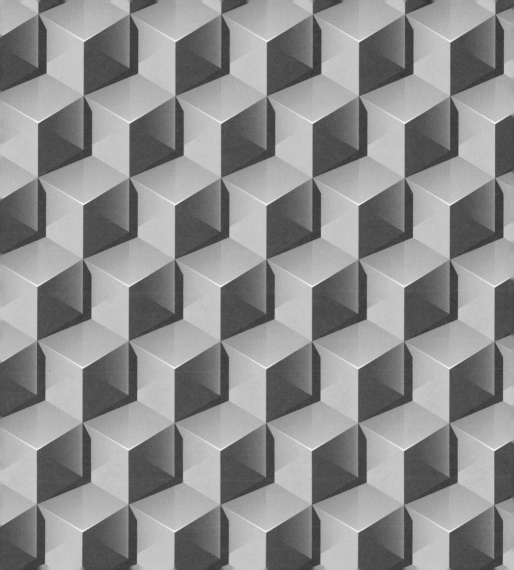

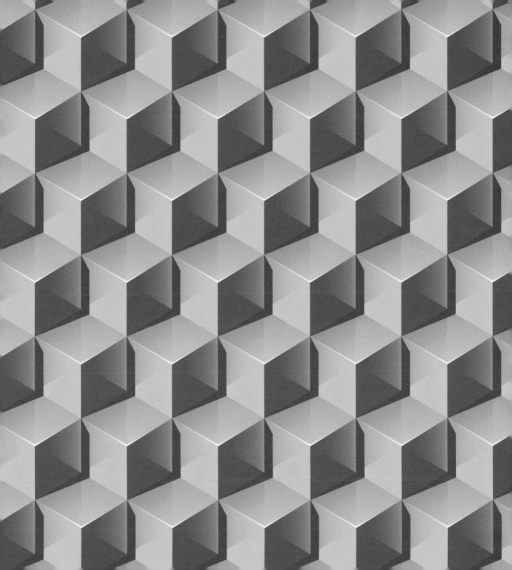

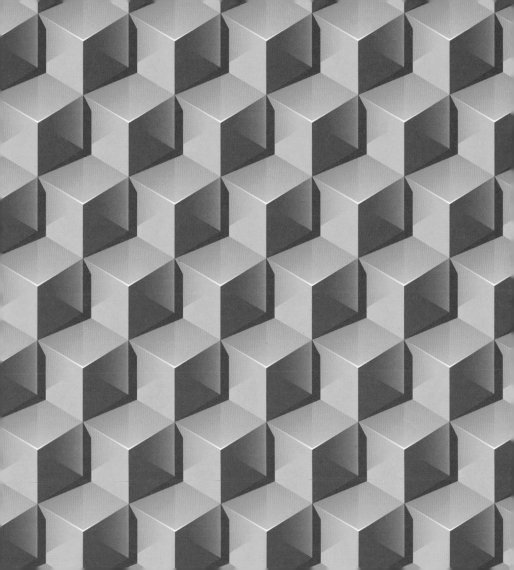

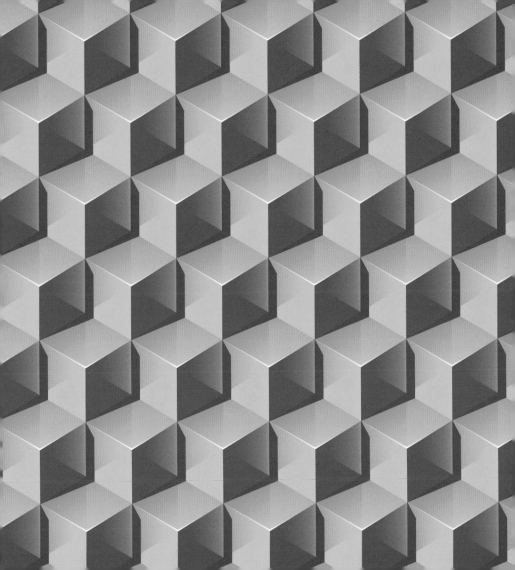

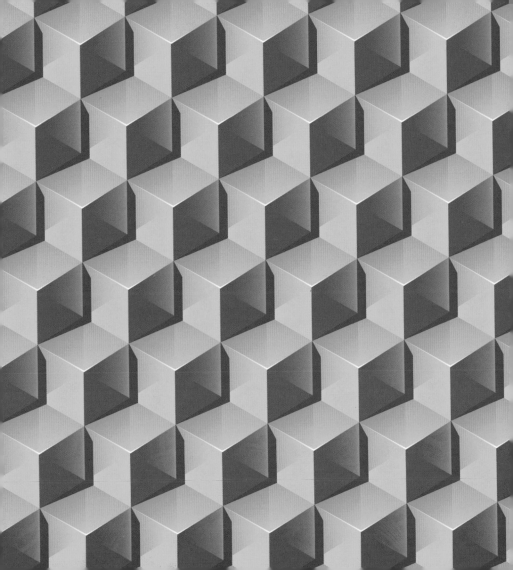

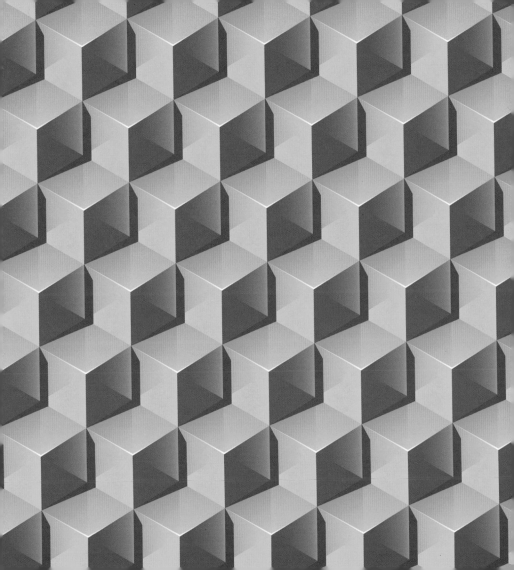

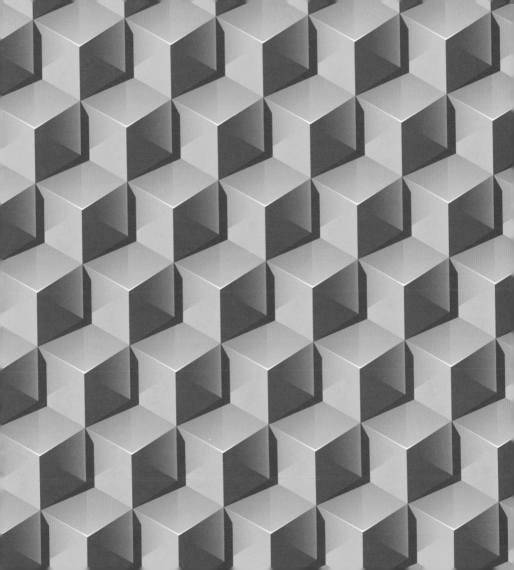

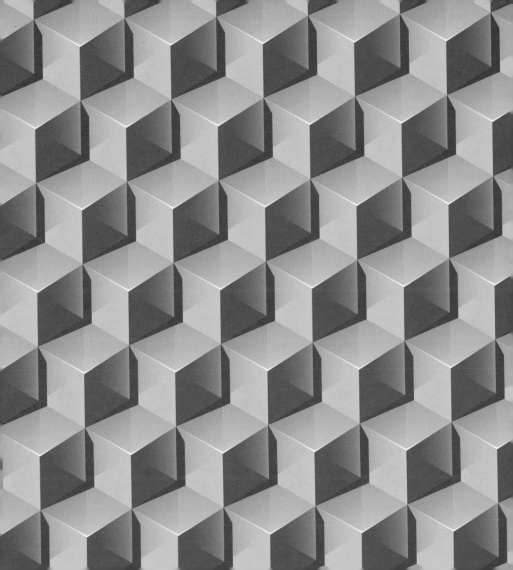

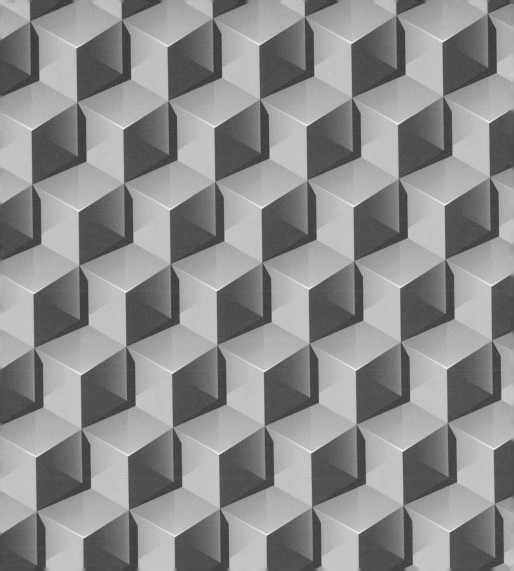

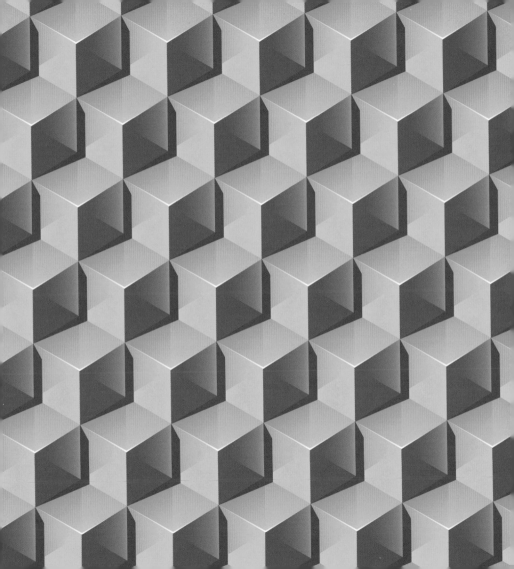

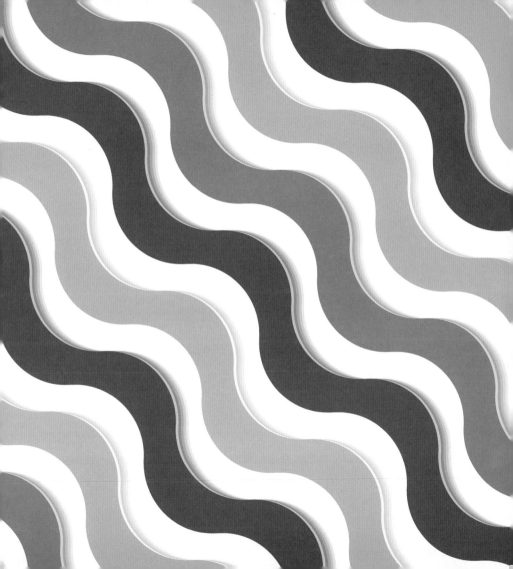

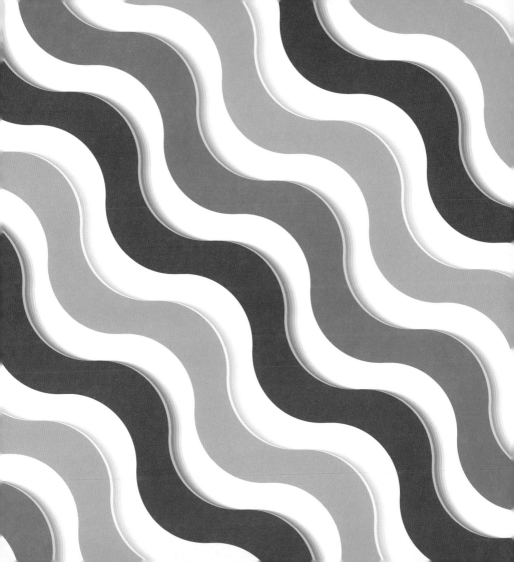

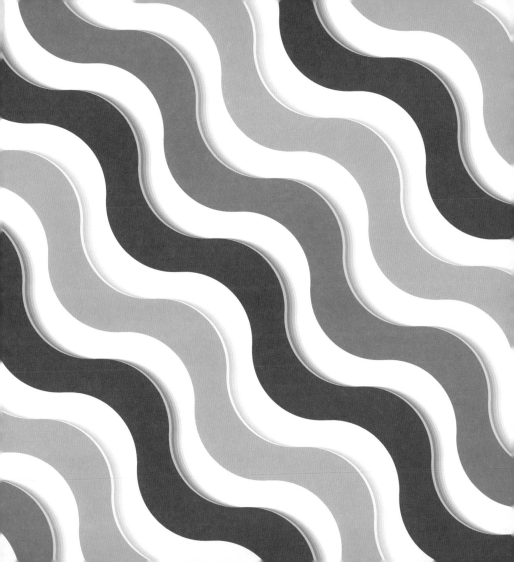

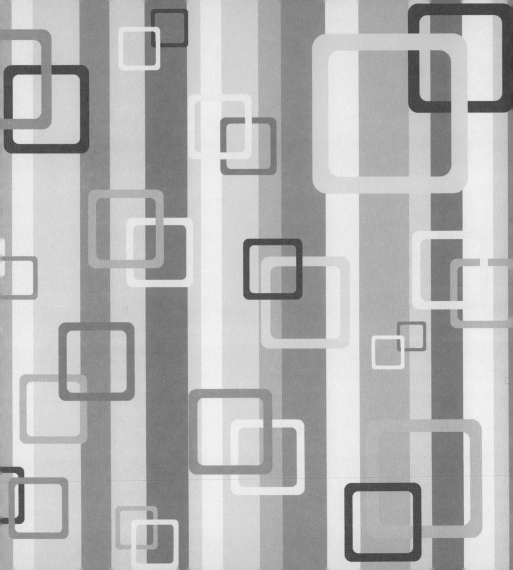

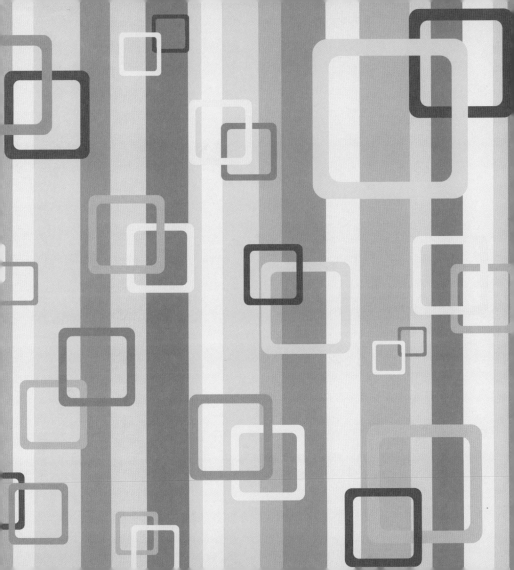

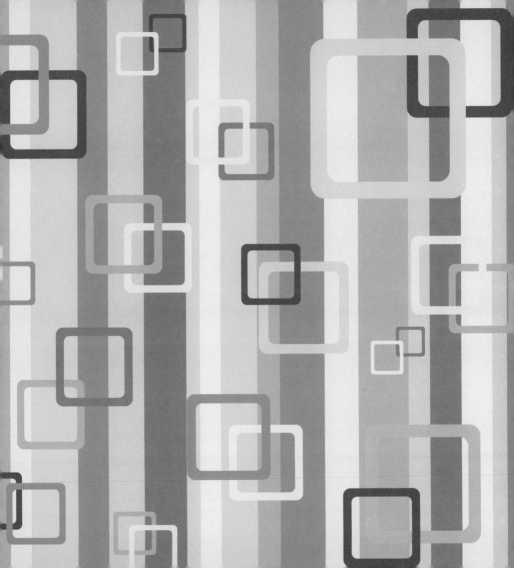

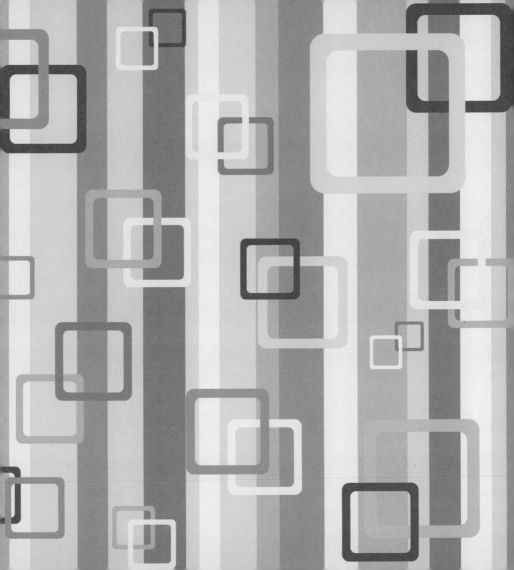

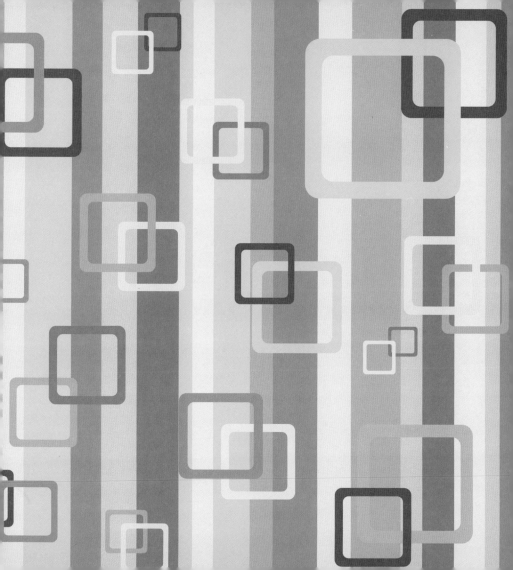

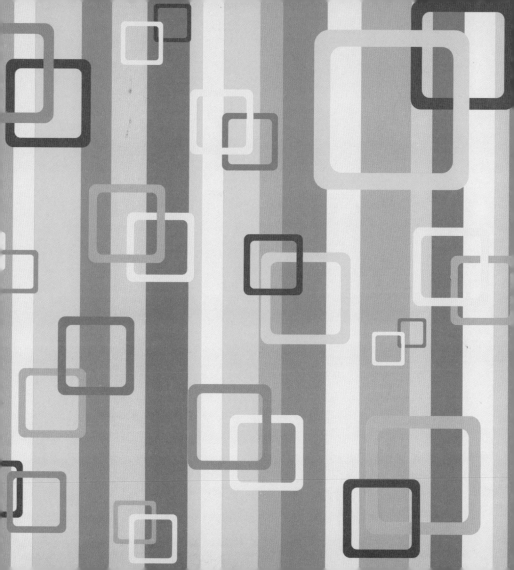

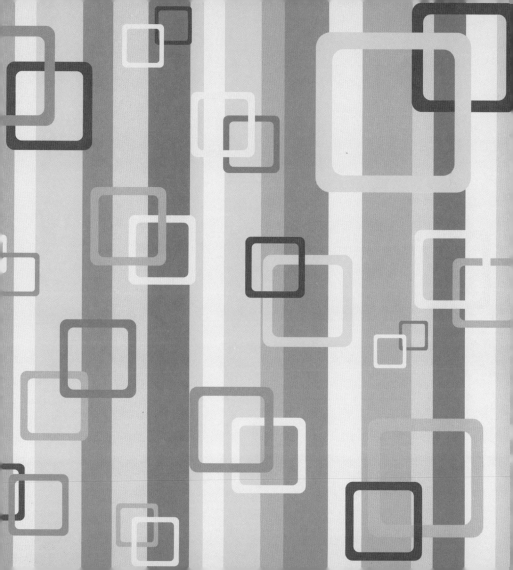

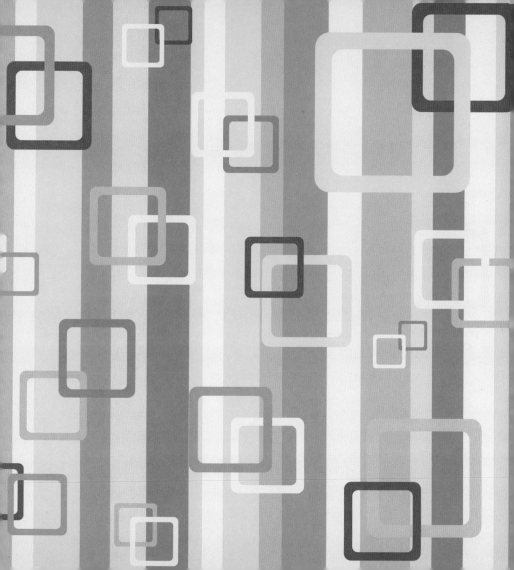

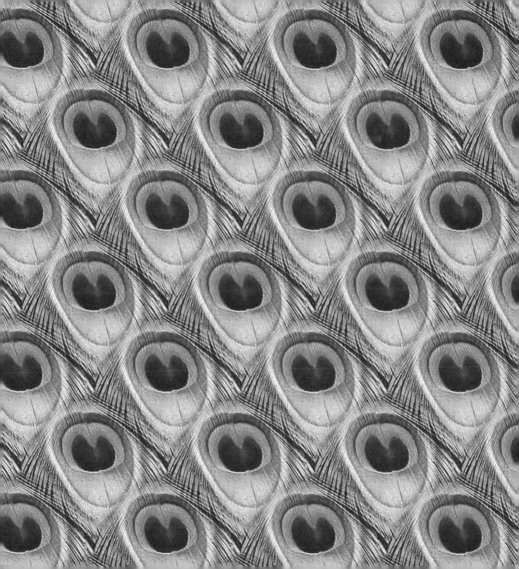

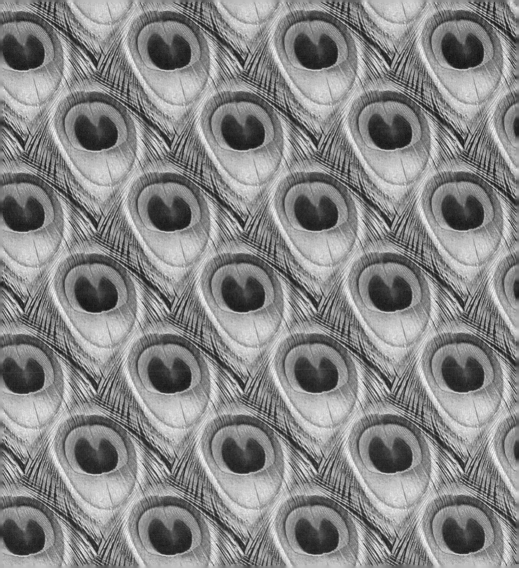

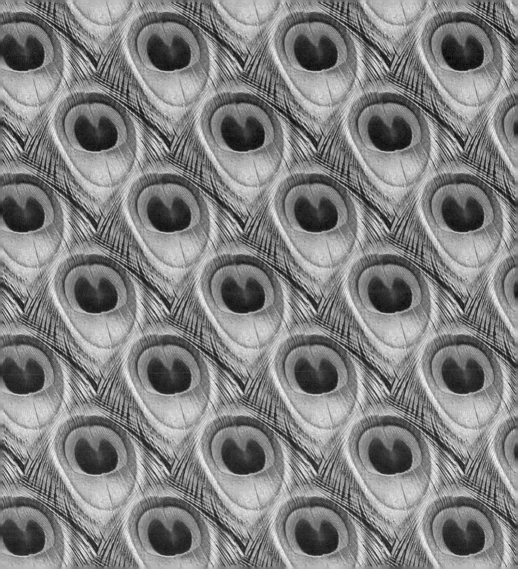

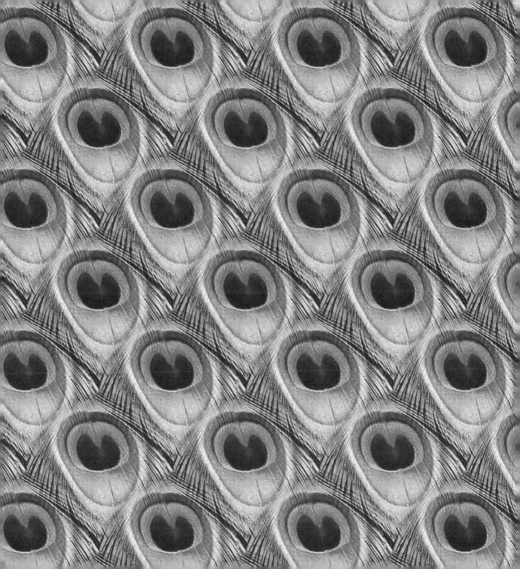

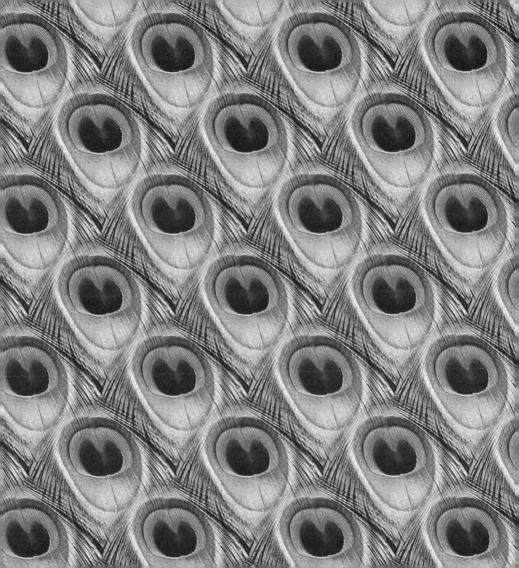

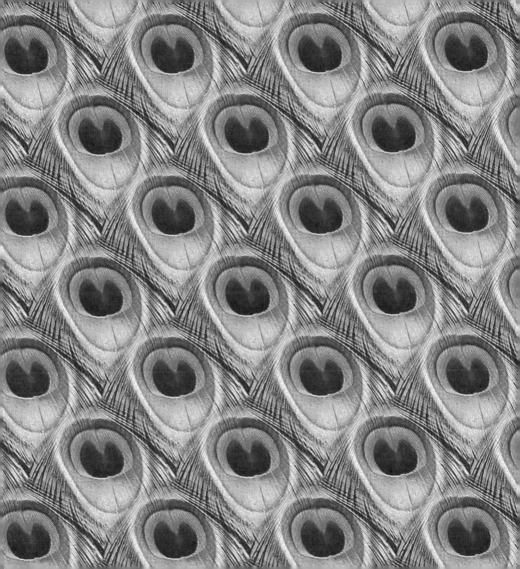

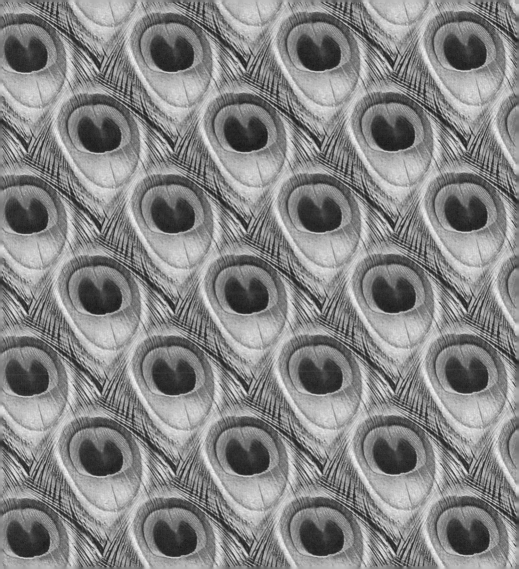

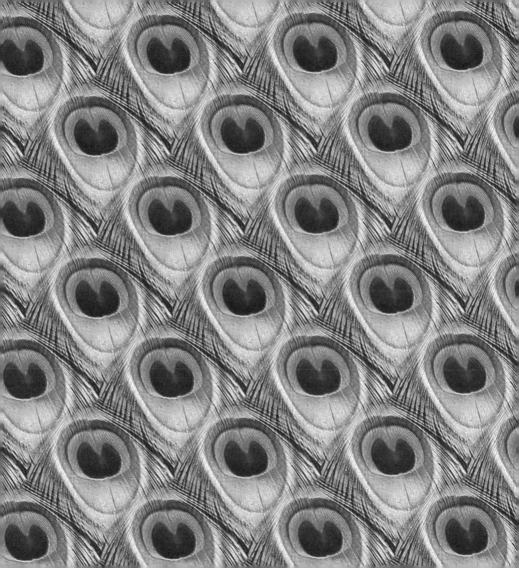

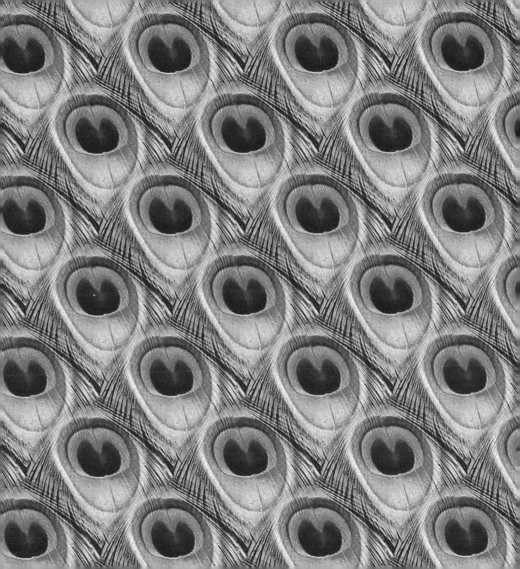

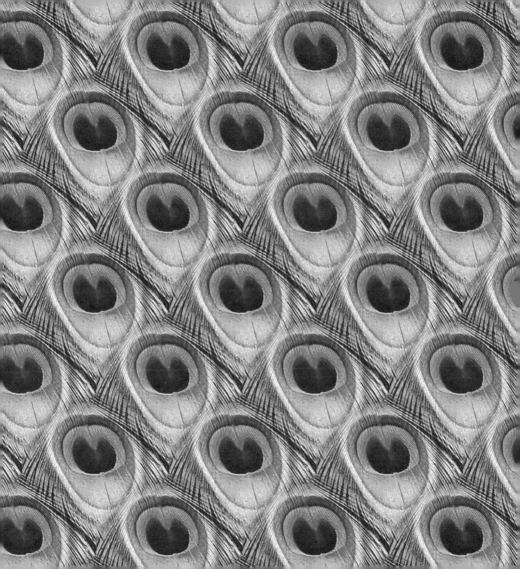

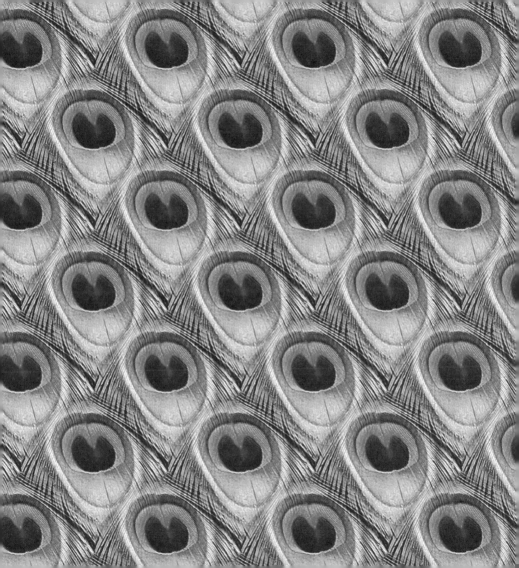

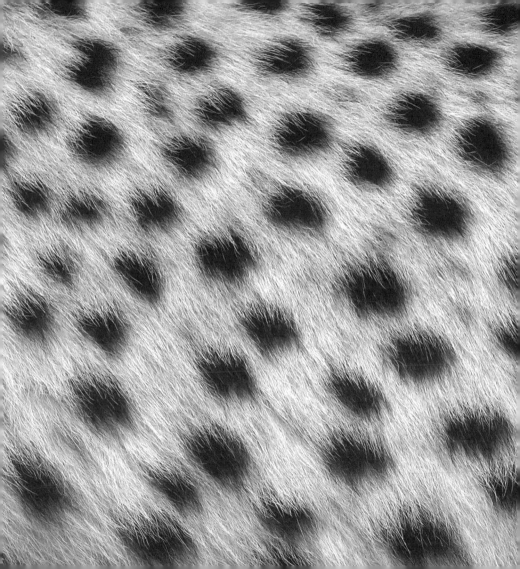

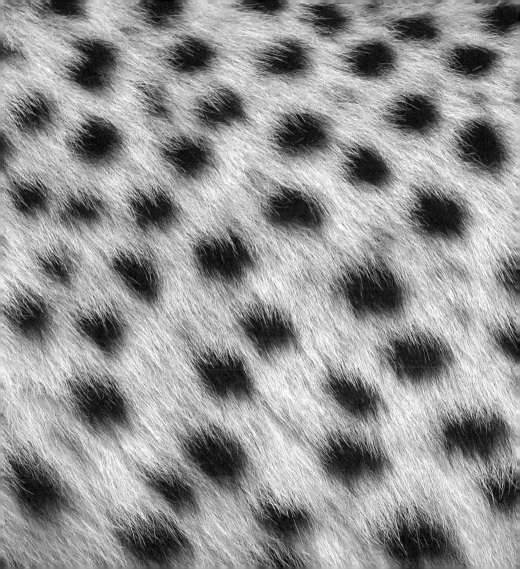

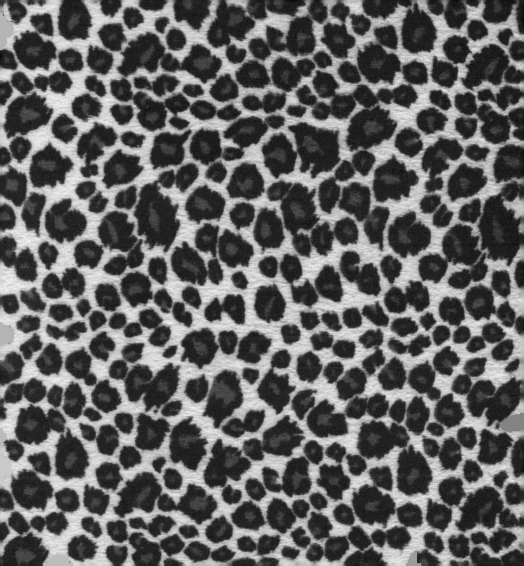

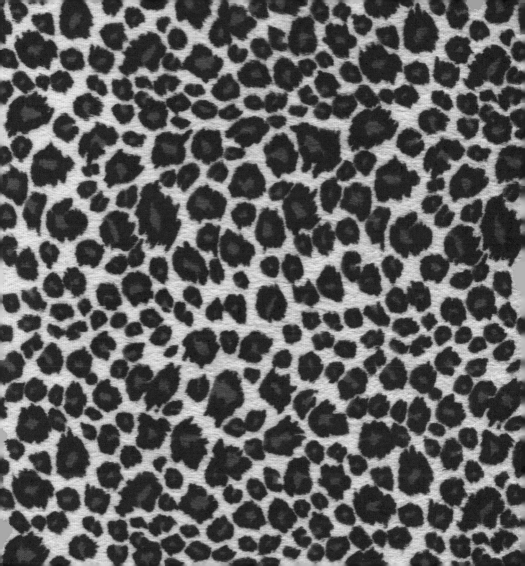

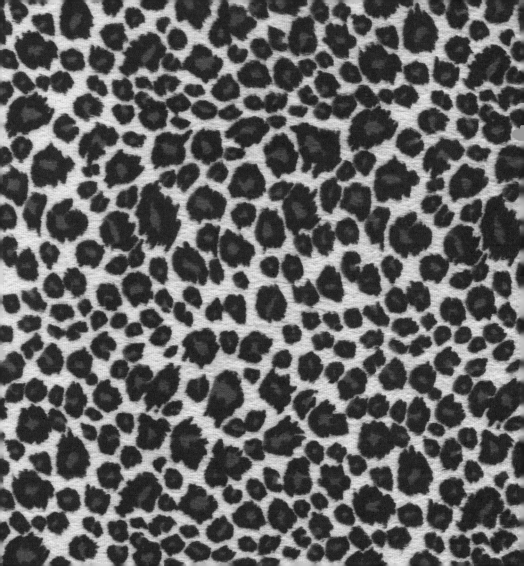

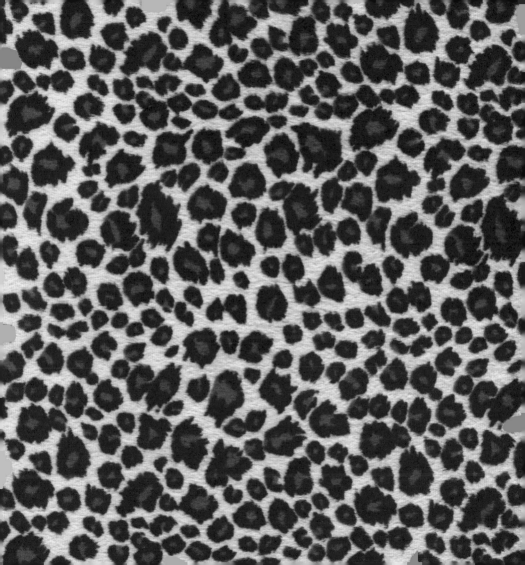

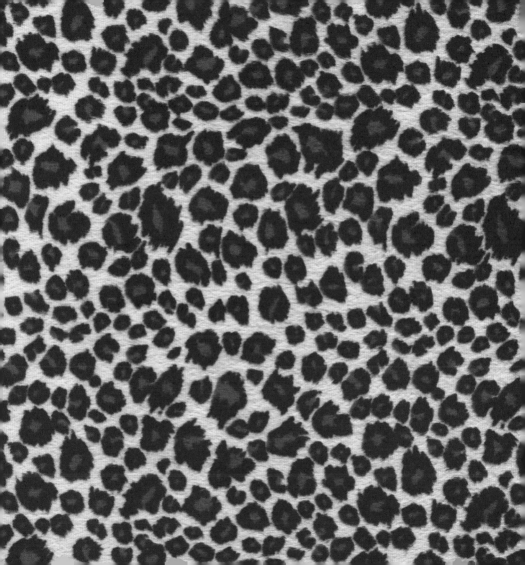

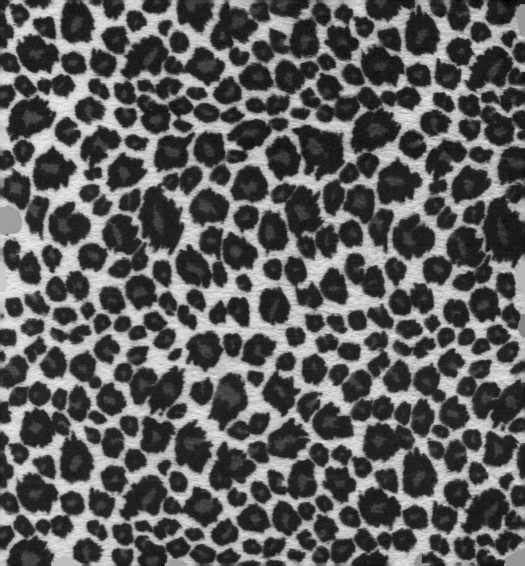

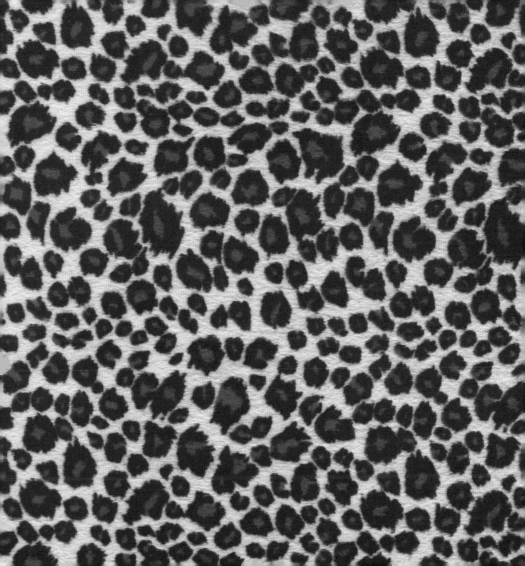

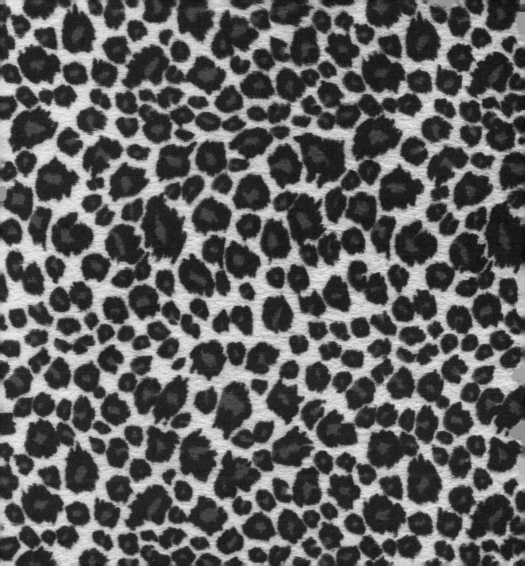

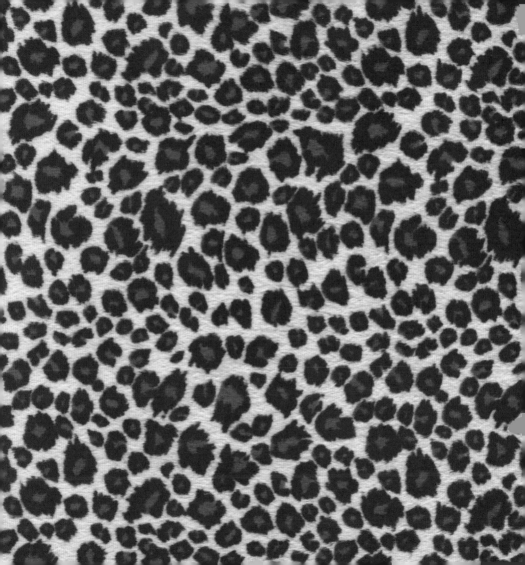

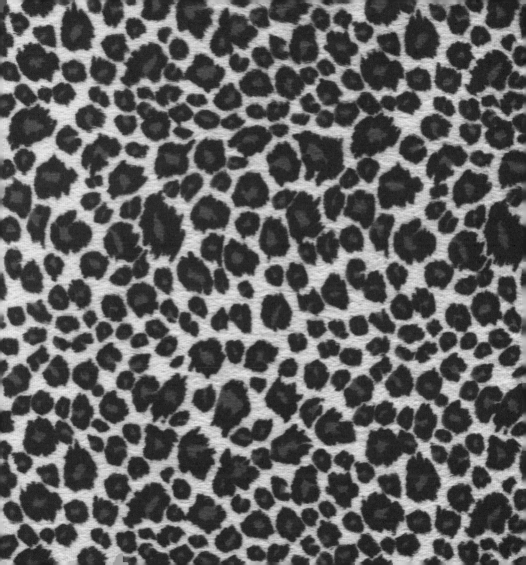

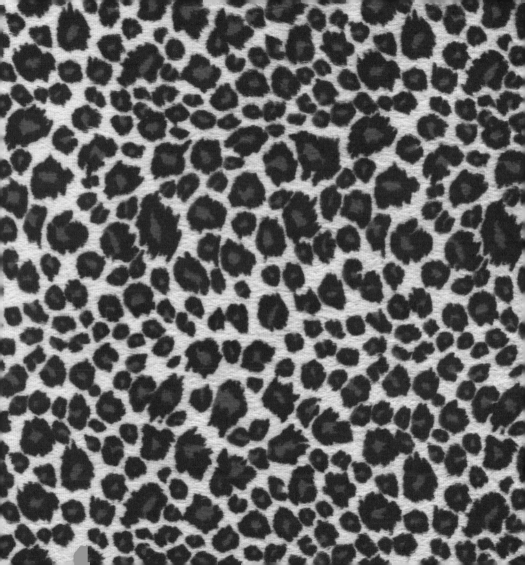

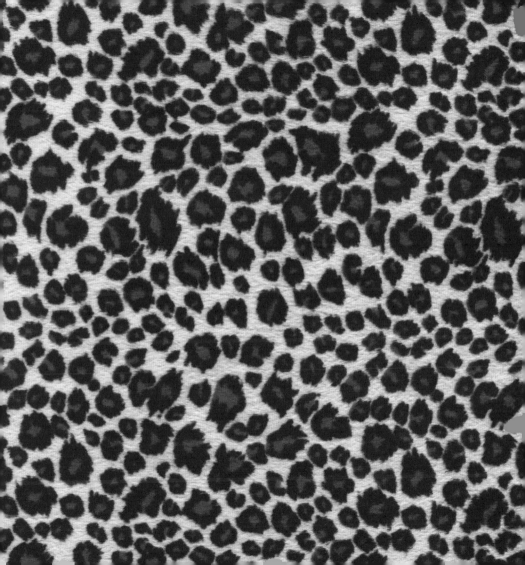

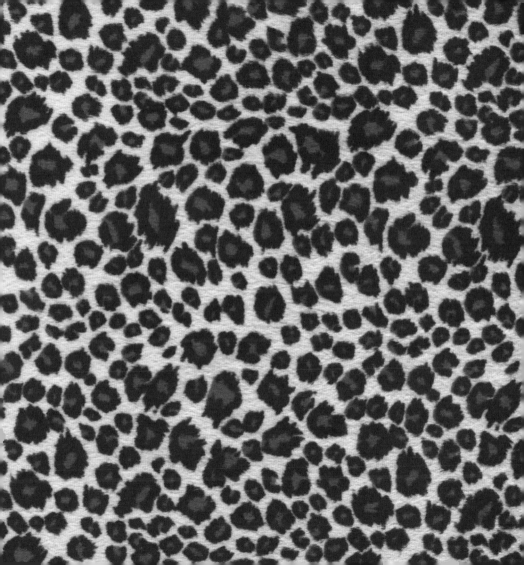

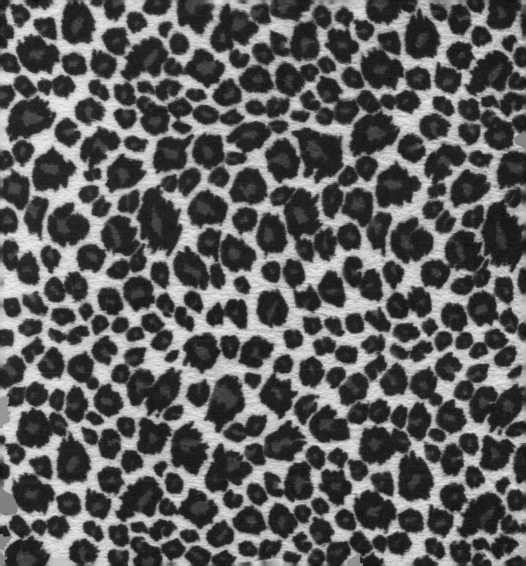

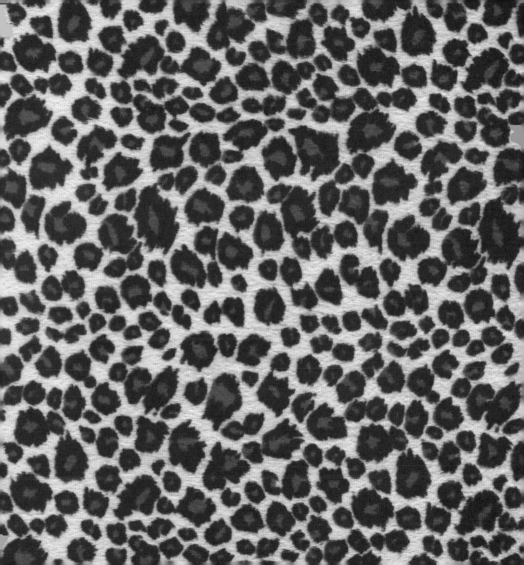

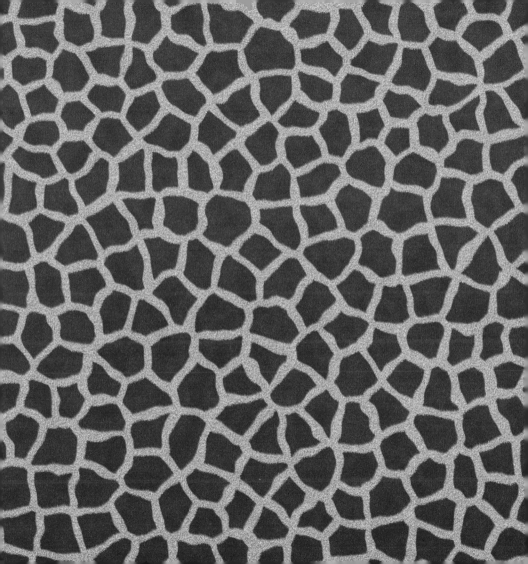

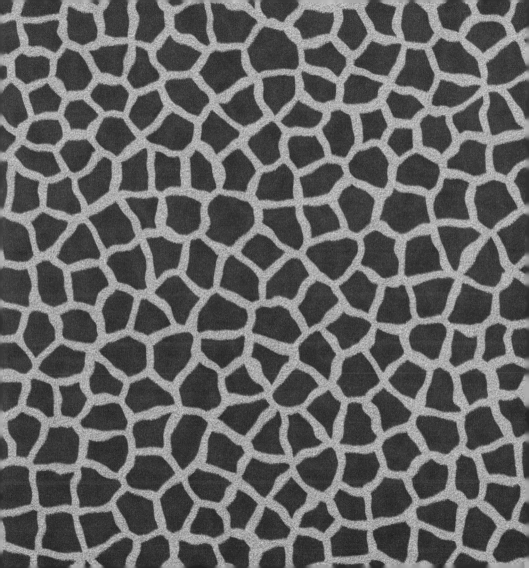

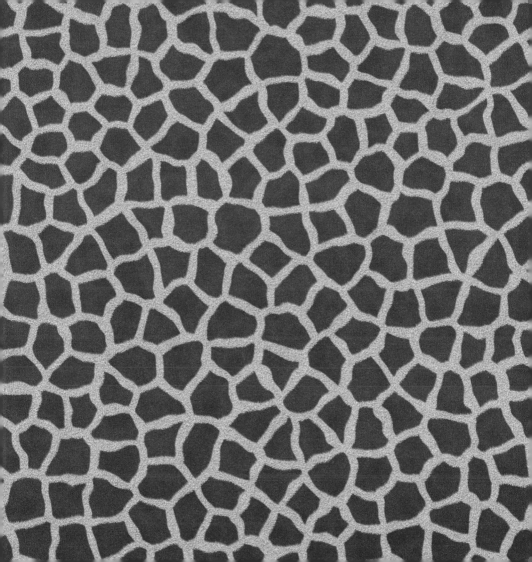

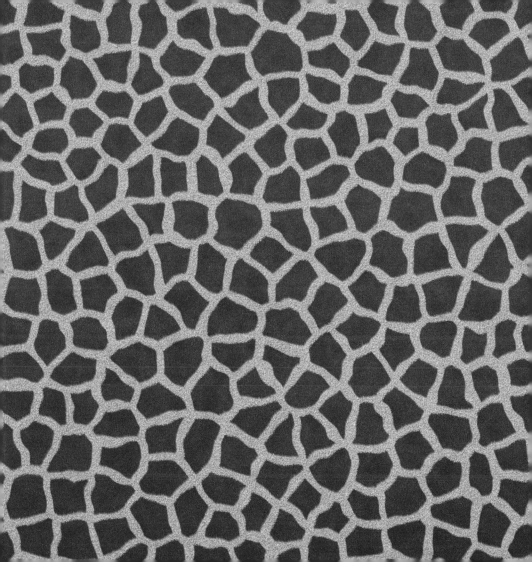

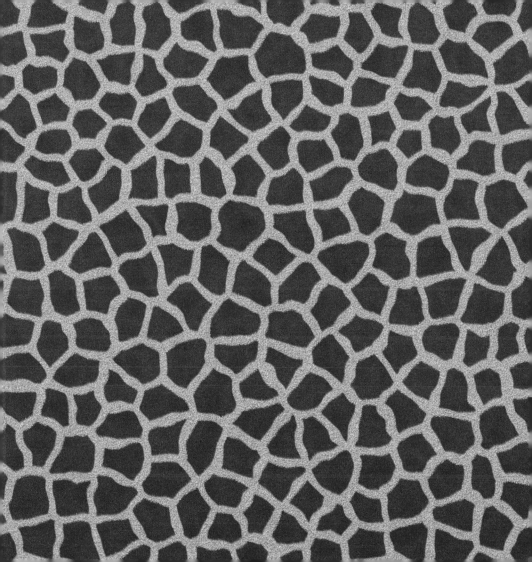

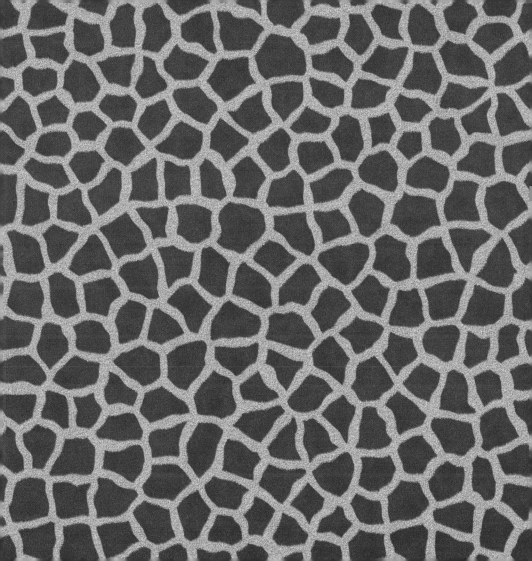